This, the flakiest **Doonesbury** book yet, is, in part, the happy result of Clyde's inability to impress girl friend Virginia with stylish new wheels. When a man goes hopelessly into hock so he can lay his hands on a Buick Electra 225, complete with 8-track stereo and fur-lined bucket seats, the last thing he needs to hear is that a Gremlin would have been a better buy. Is Clyde incorrigible? Will Virginia relent? (And so it goes at Walden West.) Herein a modern parable.

DOONESBURY

In less than five years, a remarkable new comic strip called **Doonesbury** has provoked more public and media reaction than any cartoon in the last twenty years, winning legions of loyal followers and becoming the first comic strip awarded the Pulitzer Prize. Michael J. Doonesbury and the denizens of Walden Commune appear in nearly four hundred newspapers with a readership of over 23 million.

Wouldn't a Gremlin Have Been More Sensible?

A Doonesbury Book • by G. B. Trudeau

BANTAM BOOKS
TORONTO NEW YORK LONDON

WOULDN'T A GREMLIN HAVE BEEN MORE SENSIBLE?
*A Bantam Book / published by arrangement with
Holt, Rinehart and Winston*

PRINTING HISTORY
Holt, Rinehart and Winston edition / September 1975
2nd printing....November 1975
Bantam edition / September 1976

ISBN 0-553-02733-6

Published simultaneously in the United States and Canada

PRINTED IN THE UNITED STATES OF AMERICA

0 9 8 7 6 5 4 3 2 1

SITWELL, PENNSYLVANIA. POPULATION 1,733. THIS IS WHERE THE BOY CZAR SPENT HIS YOUTH — MAKING TREE FORTS, PLAYING KICK THE CAN, BUILDING UP HIS FIRST PORTFOLIO.

THE CZAR'S FATHER, ALBERT. I'LL NEVER FORGET THE DAY HE BOUGHT HIS FIRST TEN SHARES OF COMMON STOCK. IT WAS IN A STRUGGLING NEW COMPANY CALLED *IBM*.

I HAVE TO ADMIT THAT AT THE TIME I DISAPPROVED. I TOLD HIM THE INVESTMENT WAS CHANCEY, DICEY — THAT I WOULDN'T PUT A PENNY INTO A COMPANY LIKE THAT!

THAT PROBABLY EXPLAINS WHY I'M STILL LIVING IN A MOBILE HOME.

WALL STREET. NEW YORK'S YELLOW BRICK ROAD. THE PLACE WHERE A THOUSAND DREAMS ARE REALIZED OR SHATTERED. IT WAS HERE THE YOUNG CZAR FIRST CAME TO SEEK HIS FORTUNE.

BROKERS, INDUSTRIALISTS, BANKERS, MONEY MAGNATES OF ALL KINDS — THESE ARE BILL SIMON'S PEOPLE. THESE ARE THE PEOPLE WHO WATCHED AS HE COOLLY WENT ABOUT MAKING HIS FIRST MILLION.

ALBIE ROBERTS, A FELLOW BROKER IN THE CZAR'S OLD FIRM. THE GUY WAS A BUM. HE'D SELL HIS OWN CHILDREN IF THE MARKET WERE RIGHT.

YES, IT'S A TOUGH SCENE, WALL STREET..

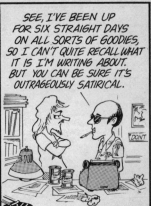

SON, THEY SAY WHEN A MAN THINKS HE'S ABOUT TO DIE HIS WHOLE LIFE PASSES BEFORE HIS EYES..

BUT YOU KNOW WHAT HAPPENED TO ME? WHEN I FELT THAT SHARP PAIN IN MY CHEST, SUDDENLY MY WHOLE **STOCK PORTFOLIO** PASSED BEFORE MY EYES — AND THE PRICES WERE **PLUMMETING!**

IN THE BACK OF MY MIND A LITTLE VOICE STARTED YELLING, "**SELL! SELL!,**" AND UP ON A BIG BOARD THE DOW JONES BEGAN TO DIVE — 800! 700! 600! 500! 400! 300!

I BLACKED OUT AT 180.

I'LL BET.

"ANYWAY, IN SPITE OF HER BOYFRIEND, VIRGINIA IS A VERY SPECIAL PERSON, AND I FEEL LUCKY TO HAVE HER AS MY ROOMMATE."

"THE FIRST DAYS OF CLASSES HAVE BEEN INTERESTING. I HAVE TWO MALE PROFESSORS, ONE FEMALE PROFESSOR, AND ONE GAY DISCUSSION-GROUP LEADER.."

"THEY ALL SEEM LIKE PRETTY GOOD PEOPLE, EXCEPT FOR ONE OF THE MALE TEACHERS, PROFESSOR LATHRAP. IN DESCRIBING HIM, THE WORD THAT COMES MOST READILY TO MIND IS 'PIG'."

NOW REMEMBER— THE PINK ASSIGNMENT SHEETS ARE FOR THE GIRLS; BLUE FOR THE BOYS!

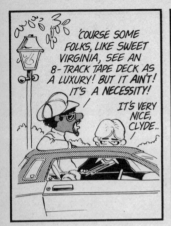

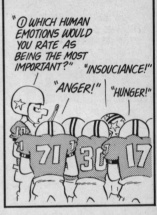

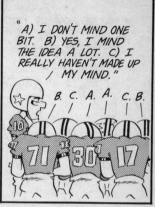

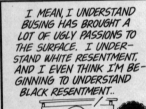

WHATCHA DOING NOW, W.S.?

WRITING MY BIO. FOR THE JACKET FLAP...

TAP! TAP! TAP!

W.S. Sloan, Jr., is a dedicated activist of long standing. He was once described by "Look" magazine as "the fighting young priest who makes a difference."

TAP! TAP! TAP!

Mr. Sloan resides in New England. He lives alone with his faithful Irish setter, Unconditional Amnesty.

TAP! TAP! TAP!

DON'T FORGET OL' KENT STATE..

..and his cat, Kent State.

TAP! TAP! TAP!

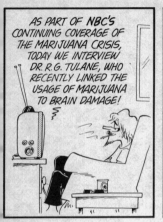